HOW TO EARN MILLIONS — WITH THE IDEALS THAT MADE AMERICA GREAT

- **STARTING OUT:** Does the business fill a real need? Have you checked the market thoroughly? Done your own research? Are you prepared to give overwhelming attention to detail?

- **PRODUCTS:** Why you should try to sell your product before you make it. . . .

- **NEGOTIATIONS:** Why the party that talks the least is often the best negotiator. . . .

- **BANKERS, ACCOUNTANTS, AND ATTORNEYS:** How to find the best—at the most advantageous price—for *your* needs. . . .

- **THE GLOBAL MARKET:** How to think global, test local, and go international—it's easier than you think!

- **AFTER YOU ARE SUCCESSFUL:** How to stay young, keep growing, and enjoy the ultimate success: knowing you did it without lying, cheating, or stealing!

===

JACK NADEL, President of Nadel Worldwide and Measured Marketing Services, has been in international business for forty years. He is the author and publisher of *Passport to Prosperity: Tales of a Yankee Trader.*

While CE National is happy to make resources available for believers, CE National does not necessarily endorse the contents or views of the authors of these materials.

HOW TO SUCCEED IN BUSINESS WITHOUT LYING, CHEATING OR STEALING

JACK NADEL

POCKET BOOKS

New York London Toronto Sydney Tokyo Singapore

An *Original* Publication of POCKET BOOKS

 POCKET BOOKS, a division of Simon & Schuster Inc. 1230 Avenue of the Americas, New York, NY 10020

Copyright © 1993 by Jack Nadel

DESIGN: Stanley S. Drate/Folio Graphics Co. Inc.

Library of Congress Cataloging-in-Publication Data

Nadel, Jack.
    How to succeed in business without lying, cheating or stealing / Jack Nadel.
        p.   cm.
    ISBN 0-671-79543-0
    1. Success in business.   2. Business—Quotations, maxims, etc.
    I. Title.
    HF5386.N25   1993
    650.1—dc20   92-39834
                                                         CIP

First Pocket Books trade paperback printing April 1993

10   9   8   7   6   5   4   3   2   1

POCKET and colophon are registered trademarks of Simon & Schuster Inc.

Printed in the U.S.A.

CONTENTS

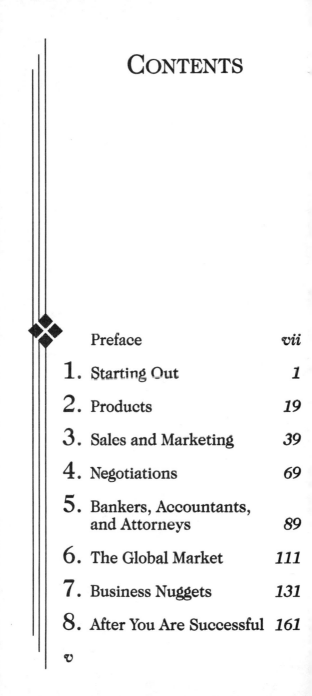

Every day headlines shout about worldwide deceit and deception. Americans are confused as old values are abandoned. We have lost faith in our leaders, both in politics and business.

Ask the man in the street whom he trusts and he will say, "No one! They all lie, cheat, and steal."

Our economy and our morality march to the same drummer. The past dozen years have seen our ethics and our fortunes drop dramatically.

An army of short-sighted executives has replaced our great industrialists. Too many of them feel it is okay to cheat as long as they don't get caught.

We have not only become dishonest, we have made everything too complicated. We are too long on theory and too short on reality.

It is time to return to the basics, to the values that made us great.

How to Succeed in Business Without Lying, Cheating or Stealing is the handbook to success. It is simple, but it packs the wisdom gained during forty years of making a fortune.

These business nuggets can be the stepping stones to a lifetime of success.

CHAPTER 1

STARTING
OUT

A STRONG SENSE OF ETHICS AND MORALITY SHOULD SURROUND EVERY DEAL.

❖ This does not mean you have to be a goody-two-shoes. Part of being successful is feeling good about yourself. You will last longer and feel better, and it's good business.

TAKE CALCULATED RISKS.

❖There is no such thing as a deal with no risk. The amount of risk is directly proportionate to the gain. When someone offers a deal and says, "You can't lose," it's probably time to walk away.

MORE DEALS ARE KILLED BY SLOPPY EXECUTION THAN BY BAD CONCEPTS.

A salesperson presents a dirty sample and loses the order. A deal is made verbally and is not confirmed in writing. The result is a misunderstanding and a possible law suit. You travel for a meeting and someone puts the wrong documents in your bag. Success depends on an overwhelming attention to detail.

FIND A NEED AND FILL IT.

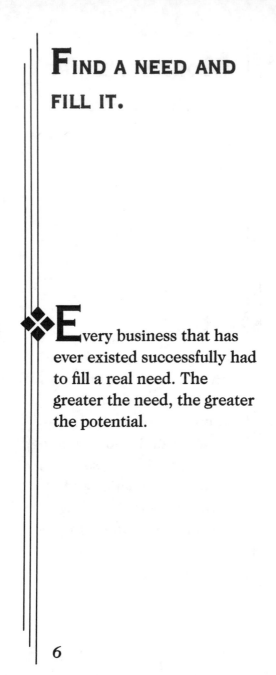

Every business that has ever existed successfully had to fill a real need. The greater the need, the greater the potential.

LEARN THE BUSINESS BEFORE YOU INVEST.

❖ **W**ork for someone else for whatever time it takes to understand the basic problems, as well as the rewards. The most expensive lesson is to pay and pay and pay as you go.

UNDERSTAND YOUR STRENGTHS AND YOUR WEAKNESSES.

◆ If you are great in sales but bad with figures, get out and sell. Hire someone else to keep the score.

TAKE RISKS WHILE YOU ARE YOUNG.

If you make a mistake, you have lots of time to recover. The older you get, the tougher it is to come back.

9

DON'T FALL IN LOVE WITH YOUR IDEA.

❖The original idea is usually born with many imperfections. It takes time, effort, and discipline to make it beautiful. Sometimes it never gets there. If you love it, you may not want to let it die. Reserve your love for people.

AFTER YOU ARE
CONVINCED THAT THE
DEAL IS GREAT, TAKE
A LITTLE EXTRA TIME
TO CONTEMPLATE ALL
THE THINGS THAT CAN
GO WRONG.

There is a downside to every deal. By looking long and hard at the negative, you are not being a pessimist— you are being a realist. If the deal still feels good, then go for it!

WHEN LOOKING FOR ADVICE, TALK TO THE GUY WHO HAS THE RECORD.

❖ **W**hen you consult with a successful veteran, you will get an opinion from someone who has been there and knows the pitfalls as well as the potential. Now you have advice from which to make your own decision. The odds are you will make the right move.

Do your own research.

❖ **W**hen you get the information secondhand, it has been filtered through somebody else's prejudices. At least at the beginning, get the facts directly from the source.

IF YOU ARE GOING TO GAMBLE, DO IT WITH A FULL DECK.

You may think you have an original because neither you nor your Aunt Tilly has seen it. Believe it or not, someone else may have had your great idea before you. He may even have gone down the tubes with it. Save yourself time, money, and grief. Check the market thoroughly before you invest in a new product or idea.

IF YOUR DEAL TAKES CAPITAL (AND THEY ALL DO), MAKE SURE YOU HAVE THE STAYING POWER BEFORE YOU START.

❖ More businesses fail because of too little capital than for any other reason. It is almost impossible to predict all the problems you will encounter in a new business. Figure your cash projections realistically; then make sure you have the ability to raise twice that amount. You will probably need it.

IF YOU TELL THE TRUTH, YOU DON'T NEED A GREAT MEMORY.

❖Many people self-destruct when they are caught in a lie. The lie is compounded when they try to cover it up. The more they lie, the worse it gets. Remember Watergate.

WHEN YOU FEEL SURE YOU ARE RIGHT, GO FOR IT!

You must pursue your goal with determination and enthusiasm. Anything less will be destructive to your associates, yourself . . . and your deal.

CHAPTER 2

PRODUCTS

A GREAT PRODUCT IS ONE THAT SELLS.

There is no such thing as an artistic success in the world of products. There is only one test. If it sells and makes a strong return on your investment (in both time and money), then it is a good product. If it creates a great profit over an extended period, then it is a *great* product.

TRY TO SELL IT BEFORE YOU MAKE IT.

Tooling a new product and investing in inventory is very expensive. If you can possibly make a handmade prototype, you can presell the product and greatly minimize the risk. If it sells, you can manufacture to demand. If it doesn't sell, your losses are minimal.

A GREAT PRODUCT NEEDS A GOOD SALESMAN — A GOOD PRODUCT NEEDS A GREAT SALESMAN.

The reality is that almost anyone can sell a great product that's properly priced. The ordinary, fair item takes sales people with super talent, and there ain't many of them.

Does it work? Will it last? Who wants it?

◆ If you can say "yes" to the first two questions and can name a big market in answer to the third, then you have a winner.

DECIDE IN ADVANCE IF IT WILL BE THE BEST OR THE CHEAPEST.

❖ **Y**ou must choose the market for your product. If it is destined for mass consumption, then you must find a way to mass produce. If there is a limited high-price market, the concentration must be on exquisite quality. You can't have both.

GREAT DESIGN IS WHEN ORDINARY FORCE PRODUCES EXTRAORDINARY RESULTS.

❖ **A** flute is a product designed to sound beautiful by the proper application of wind.

MAKE SURE THE QUALITY IS IN THE PRODUCT BEFORE YOUR NAME GOES ON IT.

If your desire is to associate your name with quality, be sure the quality is really there before the product goes to market. Trade names are extremely dependent on first impressions. Remember the Edsel. It never recovered from a bad first impression despite the millions of dollars Ford spent.

A HOT ITEM CAN TURN COLD OVERNIGHT.

❖**B**e careful of the fad that catches the public's fancy and is immediately a bestseller. If you are out of inventory when the item turns to ice, your timing is perfect. The most money is lost by the company that has a huge stock on hand when the demand suddenly dries up. Anyone wanna buy Hula Hoops?

Don't trust your mother's opinion — unless she's a pro.

❖It's amazing how many people show their exciting new product to their friends and relatives. These amateurs agree that it's the greatest thing since the invention of the wheel. If you want a realistic opinion, ask a professional in the business.

THE BEST PRODUCTS ARE DESIGNED BY INDIVIDUALS.

❖One person with real talent will outperform almost any group. It has been said that a camel is a horse that was designed by a committee.

A MASS MARKET ALWAYS EXISTS FOR A COMMON ITEM MADE BETTER.

❖ When there is enormous demand, expect strong competition from the major players. It usually takes a large investment, and you should make sure your product performs and is priced to compete.

PRODUCT DEVELOPMENT CAN BE A BOTTOMLESS PIT.

❖**Y**ou think it will be easy to make this item. The hand model looked terrific and you built it in just a few days. Then you have all the production problems. It always takes more time and money when you are manufacturing a new product. It also takes guts.

MAKE SURE YOUR PRODUCT CAN DO WHAT YOU ADVERTISE.

❖**M**aking extravagant claims for your product is self-defeating. If it does not perform as advertised, it will fall into that great graveyard of unrealized dreams. You won't get any reorders for a kite that won't fly.

SUBCONTRACTING IS THE CHEAPEST FORM OF MANUFACTURING.

❖ If you don't have a factory, now is not the time to build one. There is someone out there in this great big world with just the right plant and equipment to manufacture your product. He already has all the headaches of workers, unions, insurance, accidents, etc. You get a finished cost on which you know you can make a profit. This way you keep your fixed costs to an absolute minimum. In Italy they have a curse: "I wish you many employees."

IF IT DOESN'T SELL WITH GOOD MARKETING — IT'S PROBABLY A BAD PRODUCT.

❖ Take your loss and try again with something else. One of the toughest decisions you have to make is the decision to give up on a product.

IF HALF OF YOUR PRODUCTS ARE SUCCESSFUL, YOU ARE BATTING .500—A GREAT AVERAGE IN ANY LEAGUE.

The greatest fear is the fear of failure. When you are swinging, you have to miss a few. One of the greatest hitters in the history of baseball, Babe Ruth, established many strike-out records. If you expect to win, you must keep swinging.

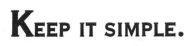

Keep it simple.

❖ **T**his oft-repeated truism must be applied to your product, its function, and its design. The customer is not a rocket scientist.

CHAPTER 3

SALES
AND
MARKETING

IF YOU CAN THINK AND TALK, YOU CAN SELL.

❖**Y**ou do not need a master's degree to sell. You must *know* your product, your customers' needs, and have the ability to present that product without getting complicated. Fast talk and slick salesmen went out with high-button shoes.

YOU CAN'T CREATE THE MARKET, BUT YOU MUST UNDERSTAND IT.

❖ No one is big enough, strong enough, or smart enough to create an entirely new market, but we must recognize the one that exists. Understanding the real needs in today's and tomorrow's markets is essential before any program can be developed.

IF YOU CAN'T EXPLAIN IT IN SIXTY SECONDS, YOU PROBABLY CAN'T SELL IT.

❖ You have just one minute to get your prospect's attention. If he does not understand you, you have lost him before you had the chance to sell him. Think of sending a telegram, not a letter. *Make every word count.*

IF YOUR PREMISE IS WRONG— EVERYTHING THAT FOLLOWS IS WRONG.

If you think there is a big market for horse blankets (and this assumption is wrong), then you can manufacture the world's greatest horse blanket—and it will fail.

MARKETING IS THE COMBINATION OF ADVERTISING, PUBLIC RELATIONS, AND SALES.

❖ **A** good executive has to be skilled in every detail that goes into the sales and marketing mix. It's like baking a cake. You need just the right amount of each ingredient inserted at the right time to make it work.

YOUR BUSINESS SHOULD BE MARKET DRIVEN — NOT PRODUCT DRIVEN.

❖ "Product Driven" is trying to sell your product whether or not the public wants or needs it. "Market Driven" means selling to the needs of the marketplace. "Product Driven" almost killed the American automobile industry. "Market Driven" made the Japanese automobile industry prosper. Your business should be market driven.

SAMSON SLEW 600
PHILISTINES WITH THE
JAW BONE OF AN ASS
AND EVERY DAY
THOUSANDS OF SALES
ARE KILLED WITH THE
SAME WEAPON.

◆**T**here are so many people who just don't know when to shut up. The presentation is great—the customer is sold. The moment to close the deal has come and gone. "Gabby" just keeps on talking. He actually talks himself into and out of an order.

SELLING IS ONE OF THE FEW PROFESSIONS WITH A BUILT-IN SCORE CARD.

❖ There is no place to hide. Either you made the sale or you didn't. When you work on commission, if you don't sell, you don't eat.

It's better to sell smart than to sell hard.

The more you plan in advance, the more you learn of the prospect's needs, the more effective you are. There is nothing tougher than making cold calls and not knowing anything about the account.

YOU CAN MAKE MORE MONEY ON COMMISSION, BUT THERE ARE NO GUARANTEES.

The salesman working on commission is the ultimate selling entrepreneur. The investment is made in time and ingenuity. No matter how much money you earn, no one can say it's too much.

THE BEST WAY TO LEARN TO SELL IS TO GO OUT AND SELL.

There is no substitute for actually doing it. The experience of being rejected may have more value than instant success. One must learn that the turndown usually is not personal. Trial and Error are the two greatest sales instructors.

A CUSTOMER WANTS TO KNOW WHAT THE PRODUCT WILL DO FOR HIM, NOT HOW IT'S MADE.

Too much technical information can bury a sale. It's like asking what time it is and being told how a watch is made. A sale is closed only when the customer is convinced the product will do enough for him to justify the price he is paying. Technical explanation of how a product is made is usually of no interest to the buyer. This applies to 90 percent of what is sold.

It is easy to sell glamour — excitement — hope. It's tough to sell insurance.

❖**P**eople are more likely to buy something that will make them feel good than to invest in protection against something that may or may not happen. If your product can offer instant gratification, you will probably make an instant sale.

PERCEIVED VALUE IS WHAT SELLS— REAL VALUE IS WHAT REPEATS.

❖ There is a real danger in convincing the customer that your product is better than it actually is. When it does not perform to expectations, you can forget about repeat orders.

YOU CAN'T SELL EVERYBODY — KNOW WHEN TO GIVE UP ON A PROSPECT.

❖ Time is money. At a certain time in the relentless pursuit of a prospect, one must realize that the sale will never compensate for the amount of time that has been spent. Go after another target.

THE ESSENCE OF MARKETING IS BRINGING TOGETHER TWO NEEDS IN SUCH A MANNER THAT THEY SOLVE EACH OTHER'S PROBLEM.

There are a number of people or companies that need your product. You must first identify these prospective customers and then create a marketing plan that will reach and sell them. When this is done, you have succeeded in satisfying their needs for your product and your need to sell it.

SELL THE SIZZLE — BUT MAKE SURE THERE'S A GOOD STEAK UNDERNEATH.

❖**G**ood selling calls for presenting your product with excitement and glamour. You must create the impulse to buy *now*. But there is no way to have lasting success without constant quality.

THE ROAD TO HELL IS PAVED WITH MISREPRESENTATION.

Abe Lincoln said, "You can fool all of the people some of the time, and some of the people all of the time. But you can't fool all of the people all of the time." Business Heaven is reached by telling it like it is.

HONESTY IS NOT ONLY THE BEST POLICY — IT'S THE MOST PROFITABLE.

There is no lie so ingenious that it will go undiscovered. After a thief is caught, he is never again trusted. Every deal calls for a certain amount of trust. Being honest begets long-lasting relationships and creates better opportunities.

"IF I LIKE IT, I CAN SELL IT" IS NONSENSE—THE BUYER HAS TO LIKE IT TOO.

It helps during the initial presentation to have a good feeling for your product. But the ultimate success or failure depends on the acceptance by the customer. You can love it like crazy, but someone else has to like it enough to buy it.

BUILD A BETTER MOUSETRAP AND THE WORLD WILL BEAT A PATH TO YOUR DOOR—AS LONG AS YOU HAVE A GOOD MARKETING PLAN.

Word of mouth is too slow a process in these days of instant communication. As soon as you are ready, a strong advertising and marketing program must be launched before a competing product can get started. Many tears have been shed by losers who had the same idea but couldn't get it off the ground.

THE IMPORTANT THING IS NOT HOW MANY PEOPLE YOUR ADVERTISING REACHES, BUT HOW MANY IT SELLS.

Institutional advertising has fallen on lean times. What difference does it make how many people you reached? The important question is, "How many people were motivated to buy your product?"

Good

**ADVERTISING SELLS
A MAXIMUM
NUMBER OF PEOPLE
AT A MINIMUM
COST.**

❖**N**ever lose sight of the
relationship between costs
and results. How much did I
pay, and what did I get back?
Find some way to measure
the results.

PUBLIC RELATIONS IS DESIGNED TO PROMOTE IMAGE.

It is almost impossible to gauge the results of a public relations campaign. It's even more difficult to decide if it was worth the time and money spent. Success depends on the goals you set and whether you feel they were realized.

THE MARKETING PROGRAM THAT WORKED IN THE PAST MAY NOT WORK TODAY.

❖ There is no such thing as a formula that transcends time. Products and concepts become obsolete very quickly in today's fast-changing market. If you are not current, you are extinct.

PEOPLE TALK THIN AND EAT FAT.

❖**F**inding the *real need* takes great skill. Everyone knows that carrots and broccoli are good for you, but they don't break sales records. Ice cream with a high butter-fat content sells like crazy.

TELL THE TRUTH. IT BEATS THE HELL OUT OF HAVING TO APOLOGIZE LATER.

❖ Morality and good business go hand in hand. Even if you are never caught (which is very unlikely), it just won't work. The first person you must be able to trust is yourself.

CHAPTER 4

NEGOTIATIONS

A GOOD DEAL IS GOOD ONLY IF IT IS GOOD FOR EVERYBODY INVOLVED.

If it's good for one and bad for the other, it won't last. It is rare that anyone will come out of a negotiation with everything he wants, but the total deal must leave each participant in a better position.

IT'S OKAY TO LOSE A BATTLE . . . JUST MAKE SURE YOU WIN THE WAR.

◆ **O**ne of the biggest mistakes made by the amateur is not giving in on any issue. When the major points are finally discussed, he has already established a reputation for being unreasonable. Then the other side decides to get tough. Each side likes to think that it won. You must be more interested in getting what you want than in being declared the "winner."

LEAVE SOMETHING ON THE TABLE.

So many people think they must get the last drop of blood out of every deal. Victims have a way of coming back to haunt the victor. The more blood you took, the greater his determination to get even.

KEEP IT SIMPLE. BE DIRECT.

❖ **M**any deals are lost when the principals get off on a tangent that is of little importance to the overall deal. By the time they get to the real meat, tempers are short, and too much energy has been spent on issues that probably didn't need to be discussed in the first place.

DETERMINE WHAT THE OTHER GUY NEEDS AND TRY TO GIVE IT TO HIM.

❖ **B**efore you can get what you want, it is important to determine what motivates the other side. The real question is what is he willing to give to get *his* wish list filled.

LISTEN . . . YOU MAY FIND OUT WHAT HE REALLY WANTS.

❖ **M**ost often the party who talks the least is the better negotiator. Look at the speaker directly. Listen caringly and patiently to the entire wish list. Then you have a better idea of how far you will have to extend yourself to make the deal.

FIND WAYS TO AGREE AS EARLY AS YOU CAN IN NEGOTIATIONS.

❖ A negative start usually produces a negative result. A positive attitude at the outset indicates that you are reasonable and sympathetic to the needs of the other party. It sets the stage for getting over the thorny problems that are sure to come later.

CONFRONT PROBLEMS SQUARELY. THEY WON'T JUST GO AWAY.

❖ Every deal has certain tough issues, and both sides are aware of these thorny problems. Pushing it to the side does not make the monster go away. Regardless of the topic being discussed, it lurks in the background. You must bring this major issue into the open and get it resolved at the earliest possible moment. If you come to an acceptable resolution, the rest of the deal is easy.

AFTER YOU NEGOTIATE THE BEST DEAL, GIVE A LITTLE EXTRA.

It is very important to end negotiations on a high note. The act of doing something nice that was not necessary creates enormous goodwill. It helps to ensure that the deal will be executed with the same spirit of cooperation that existed when the deal was made.

ALWAYS CONFIRM YOUR AGREEMENTS IN WRITING.

❖**M**ost of what is said is forgotten soon after a conversation takes place. A written record dictated within minutes of the end of the meeting will preserve not only the agreement but the spirit in which it was made. Years later, if there is any dispute, there will be no question as to what was said. It's a good idea to have the other party sign a copy of the confirmation you send him, agreeing that this is also his understanding of the deal.

AN AGREEMENT IS ONLY AS GOOD AS THE PEOPLE INVOLVED.

The most important element in any negotiation is the people with whom you're dealing. The character of an individual who has been in business for some time is easy to check. Any contract can be torn apart by a skilled lawyer—and there are lots of them out there waiting for the opportunity. Be on your guard.

TRY NOT TO ISSUE ULTIMATUMS.

❖ The meekest and the weakest negotiators respond poorly when put in a corner. When you say, "This is my final offer," there is no room to back away. There are times when that is exactly the way you feel. Before you utter these words, understand that you could be ending the negotiations.

No matter how tempted you are, do not bluff.

❖ It's okay for poker. If you are called, you lose just the hand being played. In the real world of business, threats should never be issued lightly. Be prepared to execute any tough promises made . . . or don't issue the challenge in the first place.

TRY TO END EVERY NEGOTIATING SESSION ON A HIGH NOTE.

It is not only okay but it is a good tactic to take a break when the situation gets tense and there seems to be no room to compromise. Give both sides a chance to regroup and evaluate the situation. End a tough session with a humorous statement in good taste, or with some sincere compliment to the other side. The stage will be set for a better attitude for the next meeting.

Keep the door open . . . you will always want to have the option.

❖ No matter how strongly you feel that a failed deal is over forever, time has a habit of changing things. You always want to leave open the option of going back to the bargaining table at a future date.

HOW THE AGREEMENT IS EXECUTED IS AS IMPORTANT AS THE DEAL ITSELF.

❖ Everybody is happy. The deal has been made and it has been confirmed with a written contract. Now is the time to make sure all the wheels are in motion to carry out not only the letter but also the spirit of the deal. Attention to detail ensures success.

Don't let your ego get in the way.

❖ Try to give the opposition some credit for having ideas that made the deal work. You know it was your concept from the beginning, and it is not important if anyone else knows it. Take the cash. Let the other guy get the credit.

CHAPTER 5

BANKERS,
ACCOUNTANTS,
AND
ATTORNEYS

ALL BANKS ARE NOT CREATED EQUAL.

❖**B**anks come in all sizes and descriptions. Never try to change them. It can't be done. Some are perfect for the small service companies. Others are slanted to big manufacturers. Still others build their services around the global market. Proper research will reveal the right bank for you. The choice is the customer's.

ALL INTEREST RATES ARE NEGOTIABLE.

❖ **N**ot all customers of the bank get the same interest rate. The prime rate or sometimes even better is granted to preferred customers. These are large accounts with excellent credit. It's up to you to negotiate the best rate. This would also apply to terms. The first proposal the bank makes is not necessarily the best. If the bank is inflexible, it is perfectly okay to shop for a better deal. There are lots of banks out there, and one of them may just give you the deal you want or need.

A GOOD BANKER DOES MORE THAN JUST LEND MONEY.

Making loans is the main business of most banks. Their traditional profit comes from borrowing money at one rate and lending it out at a higher interest. Banks can be a great source of information. They are in a unique position to check the credit of customers and suppliers. If they have a strong foreign department, they may even recommend trading partners in other countries. Check out all services being offered free or at a moderate charge.

THERE IS NO SUCH THING AS A BAD DEAL FOR AN INVESTMENT BANKER.

When the deal is made, he takes his money up front. To him it really makes little difference if the debt can be serviced. If a leveraged buyout is being financed with junk bonds, all the commissions have been paid long before the first interest payments are met. Most of these deals seem too good to be true. And they usually are. Don't trust them. Whether you win or lose, they win.

THE BANK WILL ALWAYS TRY TO GET THE MAXIMUM AMOUNT OF COLLATERAL.

They want to secure the loan with everything they can get you to put up: your home, your possessions, your right arm . . . even your firstborn will be cheerfully accepted. Patient negotiating can reduce these demands.

YOUR BANKER NEEDS A CASH FLOW PROJECTION — YOU CANNOT BE TOO CONSERVATIVE.

❖ If you are optimistic in your projections, the loan that is made will not carry you as long as it is needed. Then you will have to go back to the bank to borrow more money. It becomes difficult to raise your credit line. You underestimated your needs, and there is now a lack of credibility. It is much better to get a higher credit line than you need, even if it costs a little more.

BANKERS HATE SURPRISES.

❖**R**egardless of the problem, you must confront it as early as possible. It must be resolved before it gets overwhelming. The worst scenario is to run out of money and watch helplessly as your checks begin to bounce. At that point, it becomes almost impossible to do anything constructive. When properly presented—before it becomes an emergency—your banker will do anything within his power to help you out of the mess. The last thing he wants to do is call in your loan.

TAX LAWS ARE NOT LOGICAL . . . NOR ARE THEY NECESSARILY FAIR.

❖**Y**our accountant must not only interpret the Internal Revenue Service but deal with each state and local government where you do business. Each tax authority has its own rules and standards. Even within a department, each examiner has his own ideas as to how each problem should be treated.

A GOOD ACCOUNTANT IS NOT JUST A SCOREKEEPER.

❖He is your key to the whole bewildering world of finance. As a business grows, it gets more complicated. You are faced with the need to produce financial statements, projections, cash flow, and balance sheets. There is the constant demand from your bank, as well as your creditors, to convince them that you are solvent and a good risk. This is to say nothing of the many tax issues you have to face. A good accountant will lead you through this jungle and keep you out of trouble.

ACCOUNTING CAN BE AS MUCH OF AN ART AS IT IS A SCIENCE.

The same figures can be presented many different ways and can be interpreted one way or another. Even tax experts can't always make up their minds as to how the same figures should be treated. Just deciphering tax laws, and getting the best treatment, is an art.

NEVER TALK TO A TAX EXAMINER WITHOUT YOUR ACCOUNTANT PRESENT. BETTER STILL, DON'T TALK TO HIM AT ALL.

Tax people have a language all their own. Ordinary civilians can go bonkers trying to reason with them or even to understand why they are so intransigent. A good accountant understands the language and has the patience to deal with them. He may even get the tax guy to accept your position.

YOU NEVER KNOW HOW GOOD YOUR ACCOUNTANT IS UNTIL YOU HAVE BEEN CHALLENGED BY THE INTERNAL REVENUE SERVICE.

There are few things in the business world to rival the dismay you feel when the notice arrives that your tax return is being reviewed. Now is the time for your accountant to come riding to the rescue like the Lone Ranger. It is up to him to prove that all the deductions were correct. You never win when you confront the tax authorities. If the damages are minimal, your accountant deserves a medal. If the results are a disaster, he deserves to be fired.

LAWYERS AND ACCOUNTANTS, LIKE TAXI DRIVERS, LIKE TO KEEP THE METER RUNNING.

It is very much in order to check all the bills from your accountant and your lawyer. You are usually charged by the hour. It is up to you to decide whether all the time spent on your affairs was really necessary. Were you telling irrelevant stories and being charged $300 per hour for being sociable? It is almost impossible to get the details on all of the time being charged. However, the mere act of questioning the charges keeps them down.

THE CHIEF FUNCTION OF YOUR ATTORNEY IS TO PROTECT AND ADVISE.

It is up to you to set policy and standards. Your lawyer's job is to tell you what you can and cannot do legally. Once you make a deal, he draws up a contract that clearly states what you have agreed. You never really know how effective he is until the agreement is tested. One of the worst tactics to use is to make your attorney responsible for your decisions. When you say "my attorney won't let me do it," you are a wimp.

TELL YOUR ATTORNEY EVERYTHING BEFORE YOU GET INTO TROUBLE.

❖**O**nly you are aware of everything you do and why you do it. If you have even a remote feeling that something you did can have a negative legal consequence, discuss it with your lawyer. Even if it makes you look bad, tell everything without fear. It will be kept completely confidential. Basic law protects attorney/client confidentiality. He may come up with answers to your problems that may never have occurred to you.

AN OUNCE OF LEGAL PROTECTION IS WORTH A POUND OF LAWSUITS.

❖ Almost always, the worst solution to a problem is a lawsuit. Schedule regular meetings with your attorney to discuss your activities. The complexity of your business and the amount of exposure should determine the frequency of these meetings. They can take place once a week, once a month, or once a year, whichever makes sense. If you can avoid just one lawsuit, it will have been worthwhile.

OUR LEGAL SYSTEM IS OUT OF DATE, OUT OF HAND, AND CAN LEAVE YOU OUT OF LUCK.

The court calendar is so crowded that it can take as long as three years for your case to come to court. The expenses keep mounting. Conferences, strategy meetings, depositions, and preparation all take their toll. The American system has created the most litigious society in the history of the world, and we are all its victims. Settle the case as early as possible, even if you have to pay more than you should. Most of the time it will be the cheapest way to go.

TRY TO SETTLE ALL DISPUTES OUT OF COURT.

❖ It takes great discipline to make unjustified concessions, but it is often the best course. Most juries in civil actions favor the little guy. If you are the defendant and wealthier or more powerful than the plaintiff, you start with two strikes against you. The cost of litigation is usually far greater than the cost of an early settlement. Quite often, the only winners are the lawyers.

LAWYERS ARE LIKE ATOMIC WEAPONS.

You have to have them armed and available for defense. They are to be used only as a last resort. Once the attorneys for all sides in a dispute are unleashed, the resulting devastation can be overwhelming.

109

DON'T HIRE AN ELEPHANT TO KILL A MOUSE . . . OR A MOUSE TO KILL AN ELEPHANT.

❖ When you retain an accountant or a lawyer, you need one who is just right for you. They come in all shapes and sizes. If you are starting a small business, then you want a small firm that can service your needs without excessive charges. As the business grows, the size of your problems grows, and the complexity increases. Then you need the best help you can get. At that point, spending more can be cheaper in the long run.

CHAPTER 6

THE GLOBAL
MARKET

THINK GLOBAL— TEST LOCAL.

❖ **A** good business may have worldwide potential, but you have to prove it first in your local area. If it doesn't work at home, it won't work on the other side of the world. Prove your deal first, then spread out.

THE RIGHT PLACE TO MANUFACTURE IS WHERE YOU CAN GET THE BEST QUALITY AT THE LOWEST PRICE.

❖ Most of the time the customer doesn't care if it's made around the corner or around the world. They say that you should manufacture locally, but they buy the best product at the best price. If this were not true, you would see only American automobiles in the United States.

Seventy-five percent of the market for American merchandise is outside the United States.

❖ After you have sold successfully in the local market, it is time to extend distribution across the country and then around the world. If you are competitive domestically, you will be competitive in the global market. It is not as complicated as you think to get international business.

A GOOD IDEA HAS NO GEOGRAPHICAL BOUNDARIES.

There are very few businesses that cannot be expanded beyond the local market. A good concept or product can work anywhere in the industrial world. It may have to be adapted, but if it's successful around the corner, it will usually be successful around the world.

ADAPT YOUR PRODUCTS TO THE NEEDS OF EACH COUNTRY.

❖ It can be as simple as printing instructions in the language of each country in which you intend to sell your product, or as complex as changing the size or design to suit their standards. You cannot sell American cars in Japan unless you place the steering wheel on the right side.

It helps to understand the personality and culture of the country.

❖ Every nation has its own character. It is of great value to understand what motivates people in order to do the best job of local marketing. Differences between people can be fascinating as well as challenging.

THE BRITISH ARE CHARMING, CULTURED, AND CONSERVATIVE.

In England, traditional value is the keystone to business. The British listen politely but are slow to accept new ideas. Quality products with proven value are well received, and loyalty is a treasured asset. A handshake is taken as a commitment in this, the most civilized country in the world.

THE FRENCH ARE HARDWORKING, PROUD, AND STYLISH.

❖Loving good food, fine wine, and designer clothing is a major asset to doing business in France. A business deal is almost always celebrated with a fine meal and choice conversation. Just make sure that all agreements are confirmed with a written contract. The French are perennially suspicious and scrupulously honest.

THE SWISS ARE EFFICIENT, NEAT, AND DETERMINED.

❖**E**very home, every office, and every factory is as neat as a pin. They are organized beyond belief. The Swiss banker displays no emotion and less humor. Banking is done by the numbers, and depositors are frequently anonymous. Everything that is manufactured in Switzerland is of superb quality and precision.

121

ITALIANS ARE CREATIVE, PASSIONATE, AND EXPLOSIVELY FRIENDLY.

❖ **W**orking in Italy is like living in the middle of a grand opera. It is colorful, melodic, exciting, and emotional. Promises are often made without knowing how they will be fulfilled. An outsider has no idea of how it gets done, but the eventual product is elegant—and usually late.

GERMANS BELIEVE THAT THE ONLY QUALITY PRODUCTS MADE COME FROM GERMANY.

There is an enormous sense of economic nationalism that is pervasive in German business. To them the mark of quality is the legend "made in Germany." They are best known for conservative styling and merchandise that lasts many years.

IN JAPAN NO DECISION IS TOO SMALL TO BE MADE BY A COMMITTEE.

❖**You** rarely see Japanese traveling alone. All business decisions are made by groups that have intensely studied every aspect of the deal. Before doing business, be prepared for a very detailed investigation of your background and character. The Japanese would rather enter a relationship than just make a deal. They have a well-earned reputation for finding long-term solutions. One needs great patience to do business in Japan, but the reward is long-lasting business.

124

THE DOOR TO BUSINESS IN CHINA IS IN HONG KONG.

It is very difficult to do business with the Chinese bureaucracy. It is difficult for them to relate to a free market. Add to this that there is little or no creativity. The experienced Chinese traders of Hong Kong know all there is to know about doing business with the West. They also know how to harness the manpower of mainland China.

THE BEST WAY TO RESEARCH THE WORLD MARKET IS TO ATTEND YOUR INDUSTRY'S INTERNATIONAL TRADE SHOW.

Every industry has trade shows, most of them international. In one place are all the players (manufacturers, agents, distributors). You can see them all, examine their merchandise, and even research their pricing. The trade show is the ideal place to make your contacts and to establish relationships in the global market.

NEVER NEGOTIATE IN A FOREIGN LANGUAGE, NO MATTER HOW WELL YOU THINK YOU UNDERSTAND IT.

There are shadings to every language that are understood only by those who are born into it. Sometimes a certain inflection in the voice gives a word an entirely different meaning. Using an interpreter also gives you the advantage of a little extra thinking time before you have to respond.

WHETHER BUYING OR SELLING, WORK THROUGH AN EXPERIENCED AGENT.

It is very difficult for most people to do business directly with a factory that is thousands of miles away. It is best to have an independent agent who is a native of the country in which you are conducting the deal. He is employed by you on a commission or salary basis and his interests are your interests. He negotiates on your behalf. He also checks quality and makes sure that your instructions are adhered to.

No matter how honest you think your trading partner is, put it in writing.

❖ This prime rule applies even more internationally than it does domestically. Minutes or years later the only thing that will count is the written agreement.

CHAPTER 7

BUSINESS NUGGETS

TAKING A PARTNER IS LIKE GETTING MARRIED.

The decision to acquire a partner has to be made with great care. It is a business marriage, and divorce can be just as costly and as painful as in real marriage. You may not love, honor, and cherish your partner, but you better make sure you respect him and that he is serving a solid purpose in the company.

ALL BUSINESS IS PERSONAL.

❖ After all the facts are determined, the charts read, the computer printouts analyzed, a final decision is made. This is usually based not only on cold hard facts but the decision maker's personal feelings. No one will buy a bad deal from a good guy, but people always try to do business with those whom they like and trust.

TRUST YOUR GUT.

❖**S**ometimes instinct is referred to as a mystical element through which many decisions are made. Your gut instinct is really the culmination of all your experiences. When you have a feeling that a deal is either right or wrong, trust it. It will usually be the right decision.

YOU MUST REINVENT YOURSELF EVERY YEAR.

❖Nothing in business remains constant. Time and conditions change. New problems have to be met with new solutions. The worst excuse for poor performance is "but we have always done it that way." The most successful companies are those that anticipate change by proacting rather than reacting.

ALL EMPLOYEES SHOULD UNDERSTAND THAT THERE IS NO SUCH THING AS A STUPID QUESTION OR A STUPID IDEA.

When people are afraid to ask a question or suggest a new idea, progress is inhibited. An inquiring mind, properly encouraged, is a tremendous asset. One never knows from which direction the next great idea will come.

MONEY ATTRACTS GOOD PEOPLE, BUT PRIDE MAKES THEM GREAT.

❖ Employees need to be motivated to produce over and above what is expected. A feeling of pride in policies, products, and company creates an invigorating climate in which to work.

COMPETITION BREEDS INNOVATION.

A free market is the healthiest arena for business. Your competitors make you rise to the need. New products and lower prices for the consumer are the natural results. Without free competition, the economy is doomed to fail and governments can fall. Remember the Soviet Union.

THE IMAGE OF THE COMPANY REFLECTS THE CHARACTER OF ITS PEOPLE.

The notion that companies are impersonal is absolutely false. Think of any company that has been in the news, and a character will emerge. It is usually the combined images of all of its people, headed by the leader—say Chrysler, and Lee Iacocca appears. Most successful businesses are run by benign dictators.

CAREFUL PLANNING IS EVEN MORE IMPORTANT THAN HARD WORK.

It is in the nature of most hard-driving businesspeople to work hard. However, the strategy that goes into any deal will ultimately dictate its success or failure. Since it's very difficult to retrieve a mistake once it's committed to action, review the details over and over again. Word processors were invented to make revisions easy. Use them.

PROFIT IS DIRECTLY PROPORTIONATE TO RISK.

❖ **A**ny investment—be it in time, effort, or reputation— must be examined in relation to the risk involved. Almost without exception, the more you can win, the more you can lose. You can make a fortune gambling, but you can lose it just as easily. A safe investment may give a moderate return, but the risk is usually small.

SOMEONE WHO KNOWS MORE THAN YOU DO IS NOT NECESSARILY AN EXPERT.

❖Too many people have the idea that if someone has greater knowledge than they in a specific field, he automatically qualifies as an expert. In order to earn that status, make sure this person has a success story. Definitely not all consultants are experts.

YOU DON'T HAVE TO BE AN S.O.B. TO BE A SUCCESS IN BUSINESS.

❖ It was Leo Durocher who said that nice guys finish last. But if you examine the records, he didn't finish first too often himself. Respecting the dignity of others has never been a deterrent to success.

YOUR DECISION WILL NOT CHANGE THE COURSE OF HISTORY. LIGHTEN UP.

◆ There is a tendency to place too much importance on every move that is made. By agonizing over each decision, you give the impression of being insecure. Then, when you have a major decision to make, it is difficult to establish that this one really is important.

IF YOU ARE LOOKING FOR PEACE AND QUIET, STAY OUT OF BUSINESS.

Turmoil, excitement, disputes, and anxiety are constant. If your business were easy, everybody would be in it. The bigger the deal, the greater the controversy. "Serene business" is an oxymoron.

WHEN YOU REALLY UNDERSTAND YOUR PROBLEM, YOU ARE HALFWAY TO THE SOLUTION.

❖ Problems do not get solved when the central issue is avoided. Continuing difficulty almost always points to people rather than things. When you recognize the cause, the solution may not be pleasant, but it is obvious.

MOST PEOPLE RESIST CHANGE.

❖**O**ver the years, repetition produces a comfort level. Time and changing business conditions have a tendency to make old methods obsolete. Despite the discomfort, procedures have to be altered to meet new circumstances.

THE COMPANY MUST PROVIDE OPPORTUNITY TO ITS EMPLOYEES.

❖ **E**mployees must be convinced that they can advance to bigger and better positions. Wherever possible, promotions should come from within. The clearer this policy is, the better the morale will be.

WITHOUT HARD WORK, TALENT IS WASTED.

If you are not prepared to make the effort, you negate your prospects for success. Thomas Edison once described *genius* as being 90 percent perspiration and 10 percent inspiration.

ALWAYS TRY TO HIRE PEOPLE WHO KNOW MORE THAN YOU.

Insecure employers hire people who will not challenge them. The more real talent you hire, the greater the chance that they will help expand your business.

CONFIDENCE BREEDS SUCCESS AND SUCCESS BREEDS CONFIDENCE.

❖ The more you do, the more you know you can do. You attempt to reach greater heights each time you reach your goal. With each victory you are even more sure of the next one. It is a wonderful and rewarding circle.

A BUSINESS EITHER GOES FORWARD OR IT GOES BACKWARD.

There is no such thing as a nice, comfortable place. Time and competition do not allow it. When a company does not grow, it begins to atrophy, and failure is inevitable.

THE INABILITY TO MAKE DECISIONS CAN DESTROY A COMPANY.

✦**B**usiness becomes paralyzed when decisions are not made in a timely fashion. The window of opportunity does not remain open indefinitely. If you don't act, your competition will.

A MEETING THAT IS NOT PLANNED IS USUALLY WASTED.

Take the time to create an agenda that systematically attacks problems and explores opportunities. Set them in a logical sequence as stepping stones to a final resolution. There is no such thing as an orderly meeting put together in a disorderly fashion.

OPPORTUNITY SHOULD BE UNISEXUAL AND COLOR BLIND.

❖ We invariably think of equal opportunity as something that benefits some minority. It is really a two-way street. Bigotry denies the company a tremendous pool of talent available to be tapped.

A MISTAKE MADE THE FIRST TIME IS HUMAN. THE SAME MISTAKE MADE THE SECOND TIME IS STUPID.

Most companies can survive almost any mistake. But a company has to fail when the same mistake is made over and over again. We should learn more from what we do wrong than from what we do right.

A REPUTATION IS USUALLY WELL EARNED.

Con men are charming and convincing. The deals they offer are both logical and sensational. Take the time to check out their reputation. Try to find third parties with whom they have done business. If the trail is strewn with disaster, pay attention and pass.

YOUR TRIP TO SUCCESS SHOULD BE AS MUCH FUN AS ARRIVING AT THE DESTINATION.

The joy of life should never be postponed for the chance of eventual success. Each step along the way must bring some form of gratification. No one has a passport that tells them how long they are going to live. The pursuit of success should be as much fun as achieving it.

DEALS ARE LIKE BUSES. THERE IS ALWAYS ANOTHER ONE BEHIND THE ONE YOU JUST MISSED.

❖**D**on't despair when you lose a deal that you really thought you wanted. Most often, it is followed by another proposition that is even better than the one you thought you could not do without.

CHAPTER 8

AFTER
YOU ARE
SUCCESSFUL

GIVE SOMETHING BACK.

◆**A**t a certain point in your life, you will feel that you have amassed enough of a fortune. Hopefully, you are young enough, strong enough, and still relatively sane. Now where do you go? It could be time to give something back. Money is one gift that is always cheerfully accepted, but even more important is your time and proven ingenuity.

Pass on your secrets to the next generation.

❖**O**ver the years you created your own methodology for success. Your approach may not be the traditional methods taught in business schools, but it worked for you. If you are proud of what you accomplished, then teach it to others. You may want to join the faculty of a business school or even write a book. You can be responsible for improving the quality of someone else's life while you give yours more meaning.

YOU DO NOT HAVE TO BE A POLITICIAN TO BE POLITICAL.

❖**M**ore than ever, after you are successful, it is enormously important to be involved in civic affairs. Government is much too important to be left to the politicians. Find out what your elected official stands for. If you agree with him, back him to the hilt. If you are against him, work hard to get rid of the scoundrel.

FIGHT AGAINST ANY LAW THAT DISCOURAGES PRODUCTION OR INNOVATION.

❖ Too often success is accompanied by a desire to keep the status quo. Things get so comfortable that we just don't want to change anything. Fear of change produces laws that promote "feather-bedding" and "protectionism." Producing quality products efficiently and economically gives us the ultimate protection without stifling competition.

SPREAD THE WORD ABOUT THE FREE ENTERPRISE SYSTEM.

In the United States, we have produced the highest standard of living the world has ever known. But over the past twenty years, we have done our best to screw it up. The myth was spread that we were no longer capable of manufacturing quality merchandise economically, and that we were strictly a service economy. We seemed to forget the value of long-term planning. Free enterprise does not allow us to get fat and lazy.

167

AGE AND SENILITY DO NOT GO HAND IN HAND.

✦**S**taying involved is the key to a full life long after you have retired from active management. As long as you are current, you are young. Let those who follow understand: You have achieved the ultimate success if you did it without lying, cheating or stealing.